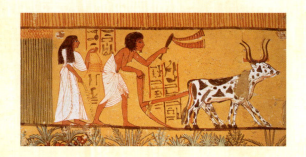

THE EGYPTIAN
BOOK OF THE DEAD

ABRIDGED

TRANSLATED AND INTRODUCED BY

E.A. WALLIS BUDGE

CASSELL&CO

3

Left The deceased stands
before Osiris, Isis and Thoth.
Tomb painting, *c.*2850 BC.
Egyptian Museum, Cairo

Above The sun god Ra in the
Night Boat, towed on the waters
under the earth. Tomb of Seti I,
19th Dynasty. Polychrome relief,
14th century BC. Thebes

Overleaf The Weighing of the
Heart against Maat's Feather of
Truth, from the Book of the Dead
of Hunefer, early 19th Dynasty.
Papyrus, *c.*1300 BC. British
Museum, London

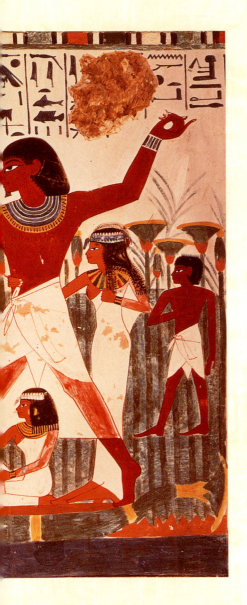

Left Fowling during the Festival of Sekhtet, from the Tomb of Nakht, Thebes. *c.*1410 BC. British Museum, London

Below Nebamun hunting in the marshes in a papyrus boat with his wife and daughter and a ginger cat, wall painting from the Tomb of Nebamun, Thebes, 18th Dynasty. Painted plaster, *c.*1425 BC. British Museum, London

7

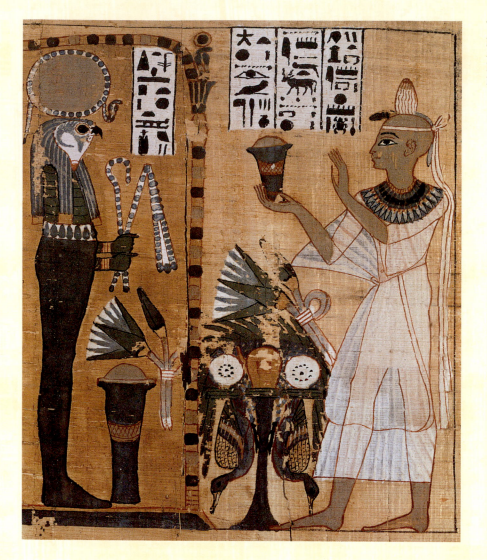

8

The priest Menkhepere
presents gifts to the god
Atun Ra. Late New
Kingdom. Papyrus.
Egyptian Museum, Cairo

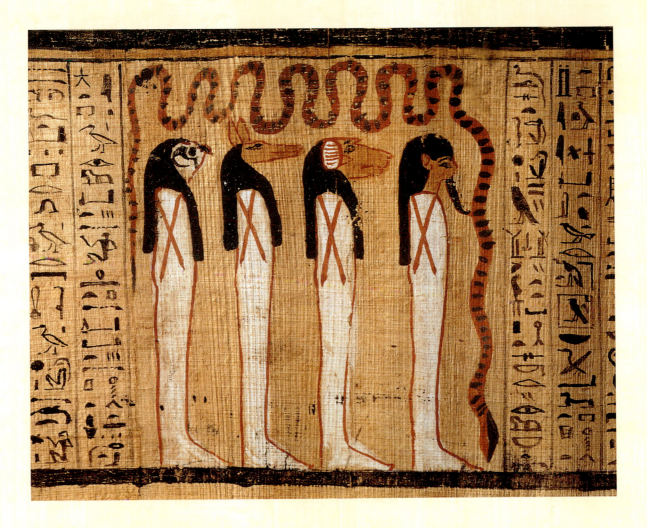

The sons of Horus: the hawk-headed Qebsenuef, the jackal-headed Duamutef, the ape-headed
Hapi and the human-headed Imsety, from the Book of the Dead of Heretwebshet,
21st Dynasty. Papyrus. Egyptian Museum, Cairo

10 The Fumigation of
    Osiris, from the
    Book of the Dead of
    Nebged, 19th Dynasty.
    Papyrus, 14th century
    BC. Louvre, Paris

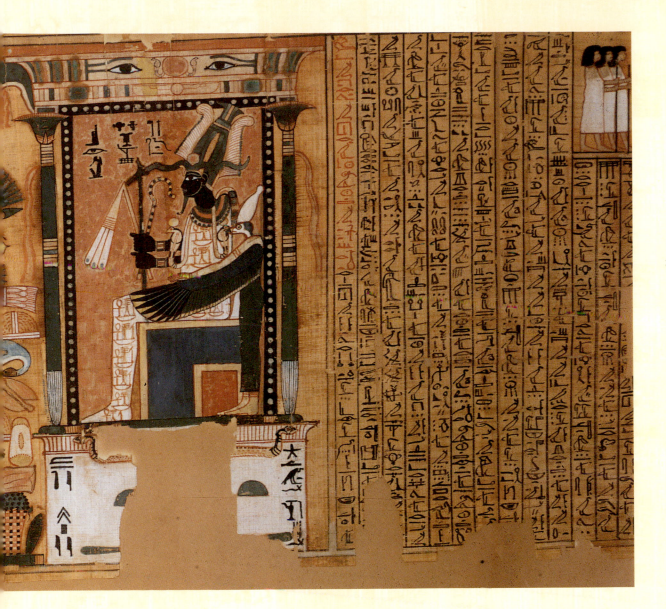

Mural painting with astronomical scenes from the tomb of Ramesses VI, 20th Dynasty. Valley of the Kings, Thebes

13

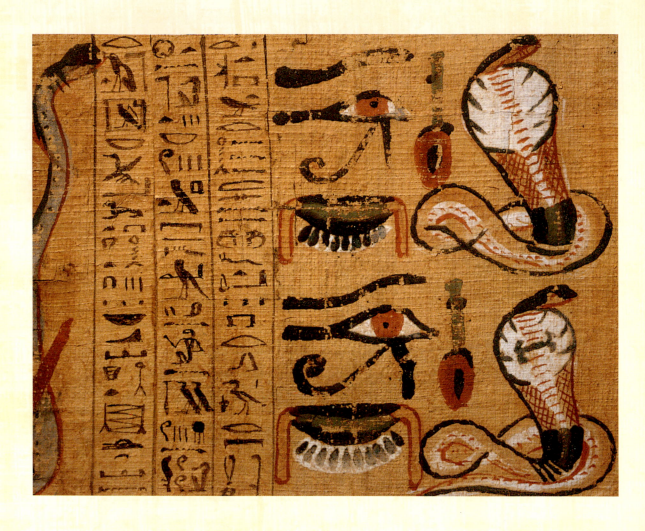

14

Above Cobra uraeus and eye of Horus, from the Book of the Dead of the Lady Herweben, 21st Dynasty. Papyrus. Egyptian Museum, Cairo

Right A woman stands before Ra-Harakhty. Stuccoed and painted wood, *c.*1000 BC. Louvre, Paris

15

Above The deceased listening
to a harpist, from the tomb
of Inherkha. Valley of the
Nobles, Thebes

Right The cow-goddess
Hathor, the eye and wing
of Horus, the cobra uraeus
and Herweben with a
perfume cone, scene from
the Book of the Dead of
the Lady Herweben, 21st
Dynasty. Papyrus. Egyptian
Museum, Cairo

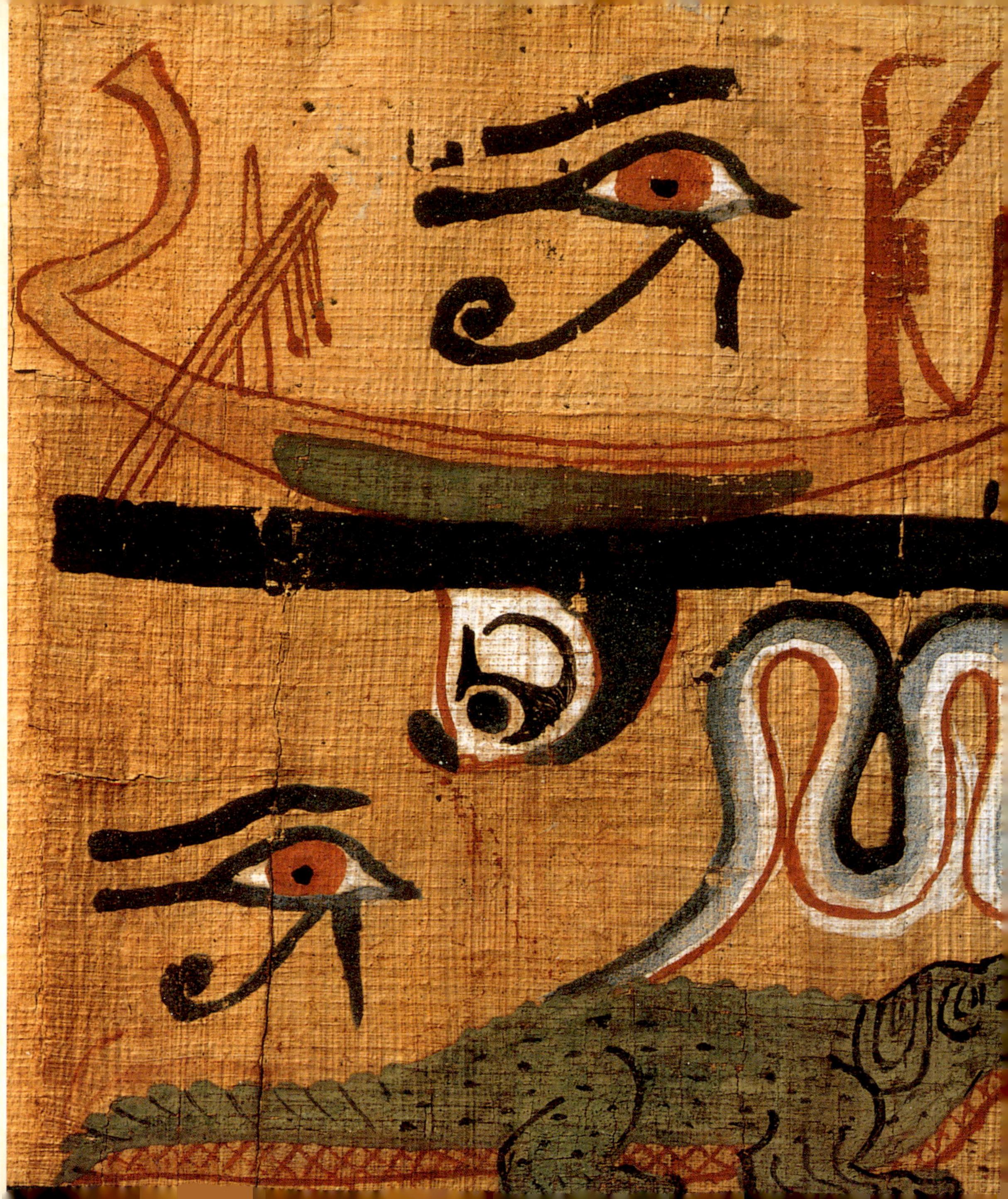

The eye of Horus,
the sacred boat, a serpent
uraeus and the crocodile
Sebek, from the Book of
the Dead of the Lady
Herweben, 21st Dynasty.
Papyrus. Egyptian
Museum, Cairo

The Weighing of the Heart. Papyrus. Louvre, Paris

The Libation of the Dead,
detail from the sarcophagus
of Amenemipet, priest of the
cult of Amenhotep I at Thebes.
Painted plaster on wood,
c.1500 BC. Louvre, Paris

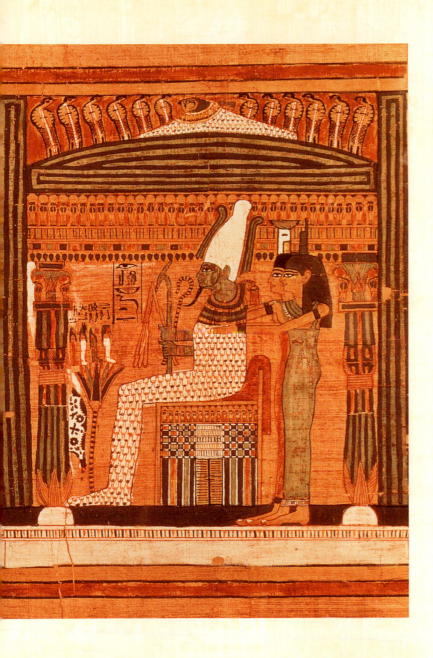

Ani led by Horus,
at left; Ani kneeling
before Osiris and
goddesses. Papyrus
British Museum,
London

23

24

Above Harvest scene on the east wall of
the Tomb of Sennedjem, 19th Dynasty.
Valley of the Nobles, Thebes

Right Detail of the
Fumigation of Osiris,
papyrus on pages 10–11

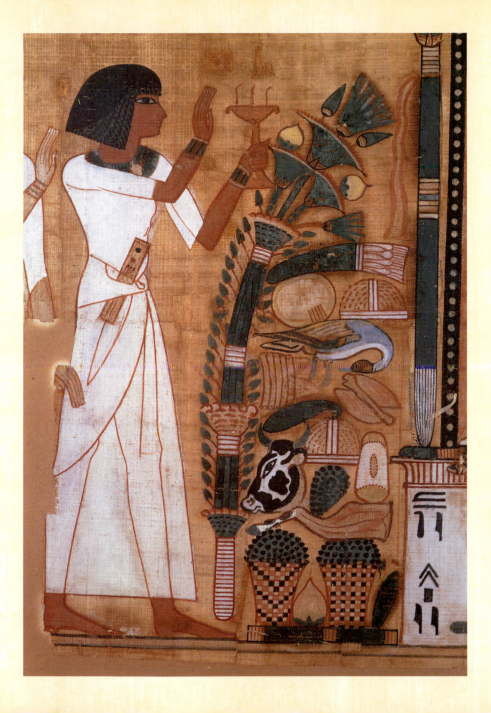

Left Sennedjem and his wife
in the fields sowing and tilling,
detail of the east wall from the
Tomb of Sennedjem

Below Glass-blowers, detail
from a tomb painting, Old
to Middle Kingdom. Painted
limestone. Beni Hasan, Egypt

Right Garden with an ornamental
lake, wall painting from the Tomb of
Nebamun, Thebes. *c.*1410 BC.
British Museum, London

Below A scarab being transported in
a boat. Papyrus from Heruben,
21st Dynasty. Egyptian Museum, Cairo

Cattle tending the deceased, scene from
the Book of the Dead of Nedjemet. Papyrus,
*c.*1090 BC. Louvre, Paris

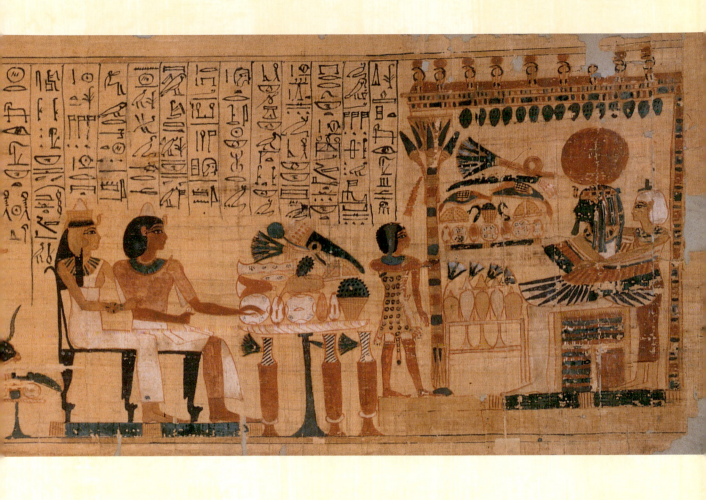

Left Herweben and her husband
ploughing with oxen and sowing
seed, scene from the Book of
the Dead of the Lady Herweben,
21st Dynasty. Papyrus. Egyptian
Museum, Cairo

Above Labourers at work,
wall painting from the Tomb
of Nakht, 18th Dynasty.
Valley of the Nobles, Thebes

Harvest scene of reaping, wall painting from the tomb of Menna, *c.*1400 BC

Right Woman watering plants. Papyrus from Heruben, 21st Dynasty. Egyptian Museum, Cairo

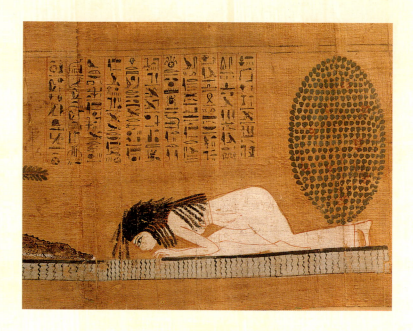

Above Woman drinking from a river, facing a crocodile. Papyrus from Heruben, 21st Dynasty. Egyptian Museum, Cairo

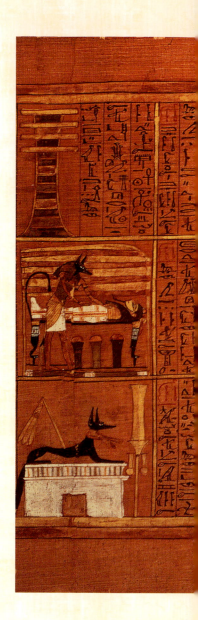

Above Female
worshipper. Papyrus
from Heruben,
21st Dynasty. Egyptian
Museum, Cairo

Right Ani and his wife with garlands
of flowers, and a group of vignettes,
from the Book of the Dead of the
Scribe Ani, 19th Dynasty. Papyrus,
c.1250 BC. British Museum, London

Above Reaping corn and ploughing, two scenes of farming in the afterlife, from the Book of the Dead of the Scribe Ani, 19th Dynasty. Papyrus, *c*.1250 BC. British Museum, London

Right Birds in an acacia tree, from the Tomb of Khnumhotep III, Beni Hasan, 12th Dynasty. Painted limestone, *c*.1900 BC. British Museum, London

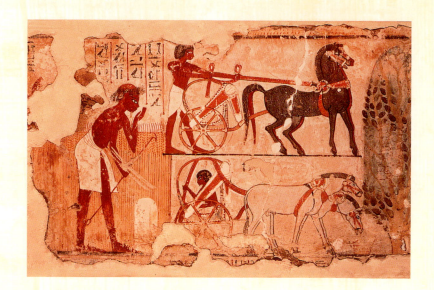

Right Horses and mules in the fields, wall painting from the Tomb of Nebamun, Thebes. British Museum, London

Below Geese feeding on grass, from the Tomb of Nefermaat and Atet, Medum, 4th Dynasty (reign of Sneferu). Painted plaster, *c.* 2600 BC. Egyptian Museum, Cairo

Left Procession with cattle and gazelles, from a tomb at Beni Hasan. Painted limestone, Old to Middle Kingdom

Overleaf Detail of a goose feeding, from the Tomb of Nefermaat and Atet, Medum, 4th Dynasty (reign of Sneferu). Painted plaster, *c.*2600 BC. Egyptian Museum, Cairo

43

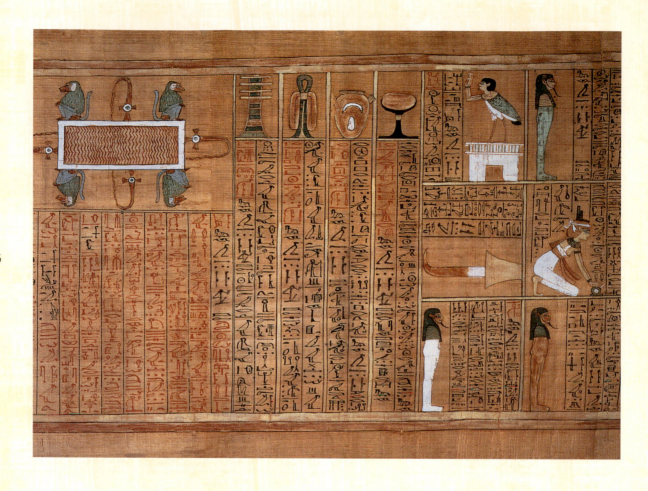

Above Hieroglyphs with depictions
of gods and deceased humans, from
the Book of the Dead of the Scribe Ani,
19th Dynasty. Papyrus, *c.*1250 BC.
British Museum, London

Right Pharaoh receiving offerings.
Papyrus from Heruben, 21st
Dynasty. Egyptian Museum, Cairo

48

Left A hawk, detail from
the hieroglyphs in the
Tomb of Nefermaat and
Atet, Medum, 4th Dynasty
(reign of Sneferu).
Painted plaster, *c.*2600 BC.
Egyptian Museum, Cairo

Above Bird and tortoise,
detail from the hieroglyphs
in the Tomb of Nefermaat
and Atet, Medum,
4th Dynasty (reign of
Sneferu). Painted plaster,
*c.*2600 BC. Egyptian
Museum, Cairo

Above Women at
a banquet. Wall
painting, *c.*1400 BC.
Bode Museum, Berlin

Right A deceased couple with their
family and servants, wall painting from
the Tomb of Inherkha, 20th Dynasty.
12th–11th century BC, Thebes

52

Left Detail of the dancers at the banquet,
from the Tomb of Nebamun, Thebes,
18th Dynasty. Painted plaster, *c.*1425
BC. British Museum, London

Above A banquet scene from the
Tomb of Nebamun, Thebes, 18th
Dynasty. Painted plaster, *c.*1425
BC. British Museum, London

A banquet scene,
wall painting from
Thebes. *c.*1425 BC.
British Museum,
London

55

Above Vignettes from the Book of the Dead. Linen mummy bandages, *c.* 100 BC—AD 200. Freud Museum, London

Left Anubis, the jackal-headed god of the dead, lying on a sarcophagus, from the Temple of Menkaure, 4th Dynasty. Wall painting, *c.* 2600 BC. Valley of the Queens, Thebes

Right Anubis, the jackal-headed god of the dead, supervising the embalming of the deceased. Wall painting, 20th Dynasty. Valley of the Kings, Thebes

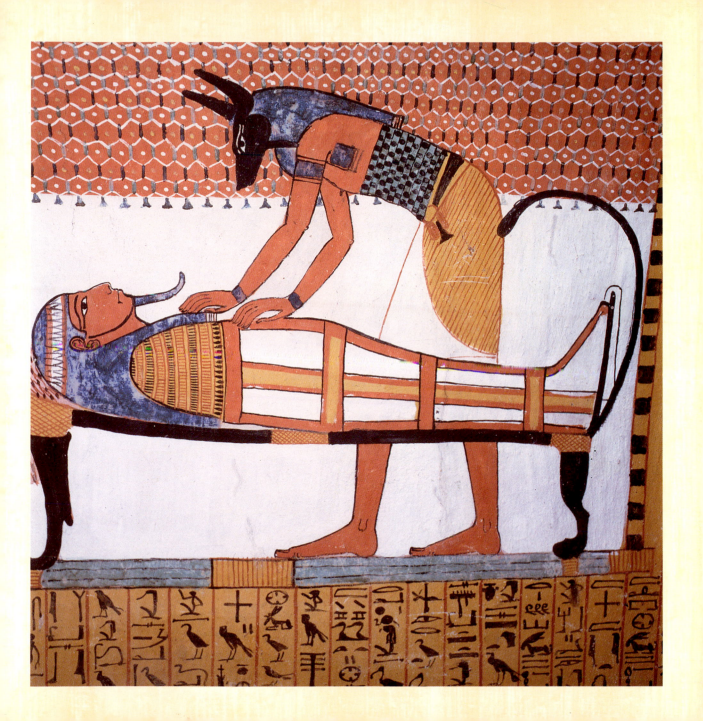

58

59

Left Female attendants bringing offerings, from the Tomb of the Scribe Niay, 19th Dynasty. *c.*1250 BC, Thebes. Louvre, Paris

Above Gods with the cobra uraeus, detail from the Book of the Dead of the Lady Herweben, 21st Dynasty. Papyrus. Egyptian Museum, Cairo

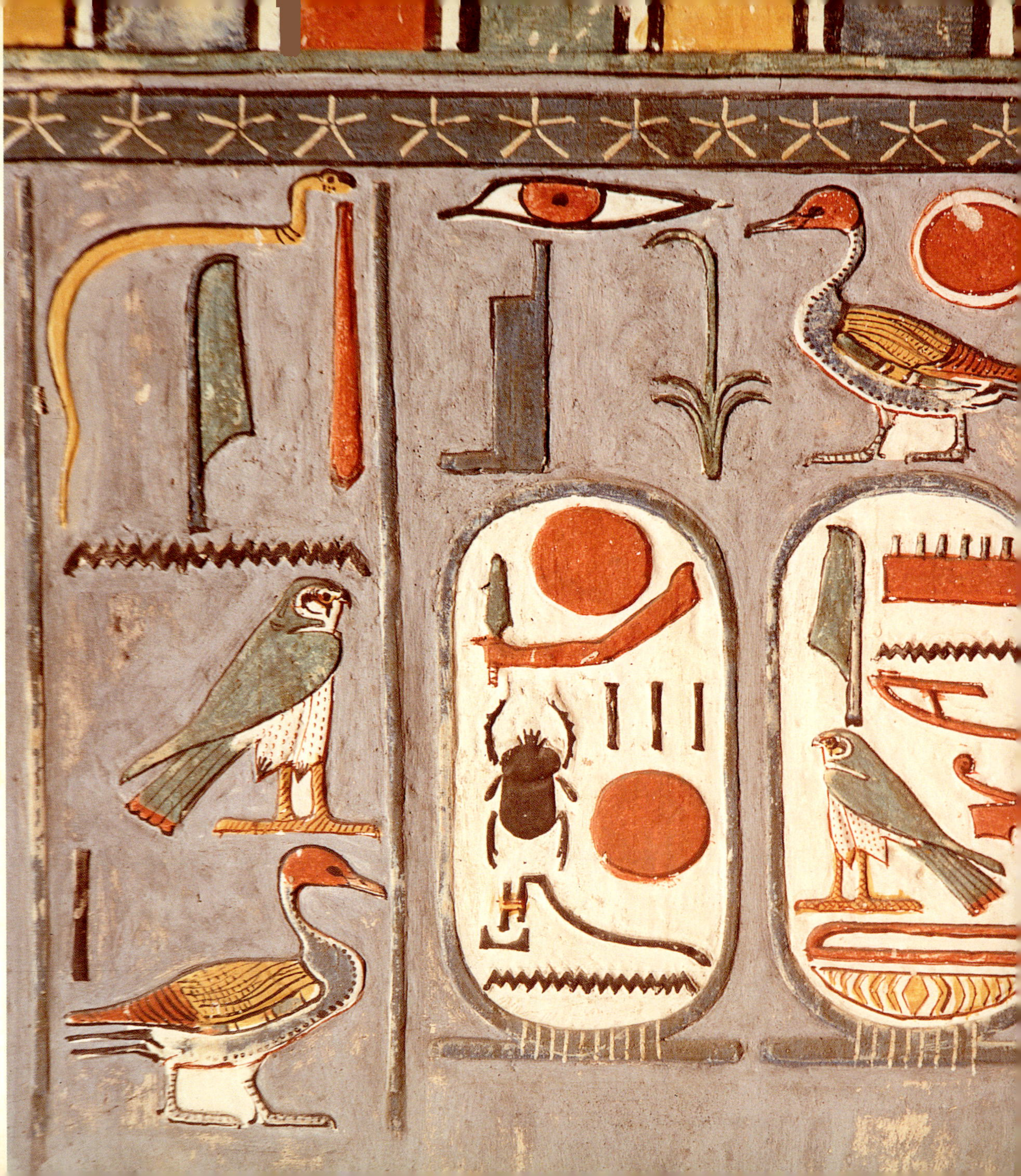

Above Pharaoh receiving offerings. Papyrus from
Heruben, 21st Dynasty. Egyptian Museum, Cairo

Left The Pharaoh's seal, with geese, a hawk
and the eye of Horus. Wall painting, 18th Dynasty.
Tomb of Horemheb, Thebes

62   Engraving and
     polishing vases in
     gold and silver,
     scene from the
     tomb of Rekhmire,
     18th Dynasty. Valley
     of the Nobles,
     Thebes

A Divine Book for the Deceased

The Egyptian hymns and religious texts reproduced here form a representative collection of the various compositions which the Egyptians inscribed upon the walls of tombs and sarcophagi, coffins and funeral stelae, papyri and amulets, in order to ensure the well-being of their dead in the world beyond the grave. They have been translated from papyri and other documents which were found chiefly at Thebes, and are one version of the great national funeral work which was copied by the scribes for themselves and for Egyptian kings and queens, princes and nobles, gentle and simple, rich and poor, from about 900 BC to 600 BC.

The early history of this great collection is shrouded in the mists of remote antiquity. The very title *Book of the Dead* is unsatisfactory, for it does not in any way describe the contents of the mass of religious texts, hymns and litanies now best known by that name, and it is no rendering whatever of their ancient Egyptian title, 'Chapters of Coming Forth by Day'. Certainly the whole collection of compositions refers to the dead and to what happens to the dead in the world beyond the grave.

As a whole, the Book of the Dead was regarded as the work of the god Thoth, the scribe of the gods, and thus was believed to be of divine origin; it was Thoth who spoke the words at the Creation which were carried into effect by Ptah and Khnemu, and as advocate and helper of the god Osiris, and therefore of every believer in Osiris, the ascription of the authorship to him is most fitting. Copies of the Book of the Dead, and works of a similar nature, were placed either in the coffin with the deceased, or in some part of the hall of the tomb, or of the mummy chamber, generally in a niche which was cut for the purpose. Sometimes the papyrus was laid loosely in the coffin, but more frequently it was placed between the legs of the deceased, either just above the ankles or near the upper part of the thighs, before the swathing of the mummy

Opposite Hieroglyphs in the Tomb of Thutmose III, 18th Dynasty. Painted limestone. Valley of the Kings, Thebes took place. In the 21st Dynasty (from 1085 BC) the custom grew up of placing funeral papyri in hollow wooden figures of the god Osiris, which were placed in the tombs, but in later times, when funeral papyri were much smaller, they were laid in rectangular cavities sunk either in the tops or sides of the pedestals to which such figures were attached. At first the figure was that of Osiris, in his character of god of the dead and judge of the underworld, but the attributes of the triune god Ptah-Seker-Ausar, god of the resurrection, were subsequently added to it, and suitable variations in the texts were made accordingly.

It was universally believed that Osiris was of divine origin, that he lived upon earth in a material body, that he was treacherously murdered and cut in pieces, that his sister Isis collected the limbs of his body, and, by means of magical words which had been specially provided by the god Thoth, reconstituted it, that the god came to life again by these means, that he became immortal, and entered into the underworld, where he became both the judge and king of the dead. His followers believed that they would enjoy everlasting life and happiness in a perfectly constituted body because Osiris had conquered death and risen from the dead, and was living in a body which was perfect in all its members; moreover, for countless generations Osiris was the type and emblem of the resurrection, and untold generations lived and died relying upon his powers to give immortality to man.

The constituent parts of man, physical, mental, and spiritual, were enumerated thus in the texts:

1. The physical body, *khat*, which was liable to decay, and could only be preserved by mummification.
2. The *ka*, usually translated 'double', an abstract individuality or personality which possessed the form and attributes of the man to whom it belonged; though its normal dwelling place was in the tomb with the body, it could wander about at

will. Care was taken to lay abundant supplies of offerings for them in the tombs.

3. The *ba*, or soul, connected with the *ka*, in whom or with whom it was supposed to dwell in the tomb, and to partake of the funeral offerings. It seems to have been able to assume a material or immaterial form at will, and is sometimes depicted as a human-headed hawk.

4. The *ab*, or heart, closely associated with the soul, and held to be the source both of the animal life and of good and evil in man. The preservation of the heart was held to be of the greatest importance.

5. The *khaibit*, or shadow, closely associated with the soul; it, like the *ka*, seems to have been nourished by tomb offerings. Like the *ka* also it had the power of going wherever it pleased.

6. The *khu*, or spirit, seems to have been regarded as a shining or translucent part of the spirit of a man which dwelt with his soul in the *sahu* or spiritual body.

7. The *sekhem*, or power, the incorporeal personification of the vital force of a man.

8. The *ren*, or name, to preserve which the Egyptians took the most extraordinary precautions, for the belief was widespread that unless the name of a man was preserved he ceased to exist.

9. The *sahu*, or spiritual body, which formed the habitation of the soul. It sprang from the material body through prayers and ceremonies and was lasting and incorruptible. In it all the mental and spiritual attributes of the natural body were united to the new powers of its own nature.

The judgement of the dead took place in the Judgement Hall of Osiris; the Judge was Osiris, who was supported by the gods which formed his *paut* or company. The judgement of each individual seems to have taken place soon after death; those who were condemned in the judgement were devoured straight away by the Eater of the Dead and ceased to exist, and those who were not condemned entered into the domains of Osiris, where they found everlasting life and happiness. There are no grounds for thinking that the Egyptians believed either in a general resurrection or in protracted punishment. The deceased whose heart or conscience had been weighed in the balance, and not found wanting, was declared to be 'maa kheru' and in papyri these words always follow the names of the persons for whom they were written.

From a late chapter we have an idea of the conception which the Egyptian formed of the place wherein he was to dwell after death. A large homestead or farm, intersected with canals, is at once his paradise and the home of the blessed dead, and the abode of the god of his city. This place is called 'Field of Reeds'. In the vignettes we see the deceased sailing in a boat laden with offerings which he is bearing to the hawk-god. In another place he is reaping wheat and driving the oxen which tread out the corn, and beyond that he is kneeling before two heaps of grain, one red and one white. In the next division he is ploughing the land by the side of a stream of vast length and unknown breadth, which contains neither worm nor fish. In the fourth division is the abode of the god Osiris, and here are the places in which dwell those who are nourished upon divine food, and the spiritual bodies of the dead.

The Book of the Dead, which was very old even in the reign of Semti, a king of the First Dynasty, was copied and re-copied, and added to by one generation after another for a period of nearly 5,000 years. The pious Egyptian, whether king or ploughman, queen or maidservant, lived with the teaching of the Book of the Dead before his eyes; he was buried according to its directions, and he based his hope of everlasting life and happiness upon the efficacy of its hymns and prayers, and words of power. By him its Chapters were not regarded as materials for grammatical exercises, but as all-powerful guides along the road which, passing through death and the grave, led into the realms of light and life, and into the presence of the divine being Osiris, the conqueror of death, who made men and women 'to be born again'.

Hymn to Ra when he rises

The deceased, who identifies himself with Osiris, praises the Sun-god Ra as he rises in the eastern sky to begin his journey in the morning Atet boat towards the land of Manu in the west.

Homage to you, O you who have come as Khepera, Khepera the creator of the gods. You rise, you shine, you make light in your mother the goddess Nut; you are crowned king of the gods. Your mother Nut does an act of homage to you with both her hands. The land of Manu receives you with satisfaction, and the goddess Maat embraces you both at morn and at eve. May Ra give glory and power, and triumph, and a coming forth as a living soul to see Heru khuti (Horus of the two horizons) to the *Ka* of Osiris, the scribe Ani, victorious before Osiris, who says: 'Hail, all you gods of the Temple of the Soul, who weigh heaven and earth in the balance, and who provide sepulchral meals in abundance. Hail, Tatunen, the One, Creator of mankind and Maker of the substance of the gods of the south and of the north, of the west and of the east. O come and acclaim Ra, the lord of heaven, the Prince of Life, Health, Strength, the Creator of the gods, and adore him in his beautiful form at his rising in the *Atet* boat. They who dwell in the heights and they who dwell in the depths worship you. The god Thoth and the goddess Maat have written down your course for you daily and every day. Your enemy the serpent has been given over to the fire, the serpent-fiend Sebau has fallen down headlong; his arms have been bound in chains, and his legs Ra has hacked off him. The children of impotent revolt shall never more rise up. The Temple of the Aged One keeps festival, and the voice of those who rejoice is in the mighty dwelling. The gods exult when they see Ra as he rises, and when his beams flood the world with light. The Majesty of the holy god goes forth and advances even to the land of Manu; he makes brilliant the earth at his birth each day: he journeys on to the place where he was yesterday. O be at peace with me, and let me behold your beauties; may I journey

forth upon earth, may I smite the Ass; may I crush the serpent-fiend Sebau; may I destroy Apep in his hour; may I see the *Abtu* fish at his season, and the *Ant* fish piloting the *Ant* boat in its lake. May I see Horus acting as steersman, with the god Thoth and the goddess Maat, one on each side of him; may I grasp the bows of the *Sektet* boat, and the stern of the *Atet* boat. May Ra grant to the *Ka* of Osiris Ani to behold the disk of the Sun and to see the Moon-god without ceasing, each and every day; and may my soul come forth and walk hither and thither and wherever it pleases. May my name be proclaimed, and may it be found upon the board of the table of offerings; may offerings be made to me in my presence, even as they are made to the followers of Horus; may there be made ready for me a seat in the boat of the Sun on the day when the god goes forth; and may I be received into the presence of Osiris in the land of victory.'

Hymn to Osiris Un-nefer

Osiris is praised as the son of the sky-goddess Nut, as the lord of all Egypt and of all creation.

Glory be to Osiris Un-nefer, the great god within Abydos, king of eternity, lord of everlastingness, who passes through millions of years in his existence. Eldest son of the womb of Nut, engendered by Seb the Erpat, lord of the crowns of the North and South, lord of the lofty white crown: as prince of gods and of men he has received the crook, and the whip, and the dignity of his divine fathers. Let your heart, which is in the Mountain of Ament, be content, for your son Horus is established upon your throne. You are crowned lord of Tattu and rule in Abtu. Through you the world waxes green in triumph before the might of Neb-er-tcher. He leads in his train that which is, and that which is not yet, in his name of Ta-her-sta-nef; he tows along the earth by Maat in his name of Seker; he is exceedingly mighty and most terrible in his name Osiris; he endures for ever and for ever in his name of Un-nefer.

Homage to you, King of kings, Lord of lords, Prince of princes, who from the womb of Nut has ruled the world and Akert. Your body is of bright and shining metal, your head is of azure blue, and the brilliance of the turquoise encircles you. O god An of millions of years, all-pervading with your body and beautiful in countenance in Ta-tchesert, grant you to the *Ka* of Osiris, the scribe Ani, splendour in heaven, and might upon earth, and triumph in the underworld; and grant that I may sail down to Tattu like a living soul and up to Abydos like a *Bennu* bird; and that I may go in and come out without hindrance at the pylons of the lords of the underworld. May there be given to me loaves of bread in the house of coolness, and offerings of food in Annu, and a homestead for ever in Sekhet-Aru with wheat and barley for it.

Weighing the Heart of the Dead

The Heart, symbol of the conscience, is weighed against the Feather, emblem of Right and Truth. The heart of the scribe Ani, who asks for judgement, is weighed in the balance and found righteous.

My heart my mother, my heart my mother, my heart my coming into being. May there be nothing to resist me at my judgement; may there be no opposition to me from the *Tchatcha*; may there be no parting of you from me in the presence of him that keeps the scales. You are my *Ka* within my body which knits together and strengthens my limbs. May you come forth to the place of happiness to which I am advancing. May the *Shenit* not cause my name to stink, and may no lies be spoken against me in the presence of the god. Good, good is it for you to hear…

Thoth, the judge of Right and Truth of the great company of the gods who are in the presence of Osiris, says: 'Hear this judgement. The heart of Osiris has in very truth been weighed, and his soul has stood as a witness for him; it has been found true by trial in the Great Balance. There has not been found any wickedness in him; he has not wasted the offerings in the temples; he has not done harm by his deeds; and he has uttered no evil reports while he was upon earth.'

The great company of the gods reply to Thoth who dwells in Khemennu: 'That which comes forth from your mouth shall be declared true. Osiris, the scribe Ani victorious, is holy and righteous. He has not sinned, neither has he done evil against us. The devourer Amemet shall not be allowed to prevail over him. Meat-offerings and entrance into the presence of the god Osiris shall be granted to him, together with a homestead for ever in Sekhet-hetepu, as to the followers of Horus.'

The Shabti

The Shabti are servant figures who carry out the tasks required of the deceased in the underworld.

The scribe Nebseni, the draughtsman in the Temples of the North and South, the man highly venerated in the Temple of Ptah, says:

Oh you *shabti* figure of the scribe Nebseni, the son of the scribe Thena, victorious, and of the lady of the house Mutrestha, victorious, if I be called, or if I be judged to do any work whatever of the labours which are to be done in the underworld – behold, for you opposition will there be set aside – by a man in his turn, let the judgement fall upon you instead of upon me always, in the matter of sowing the fields, of filling the water-courses with water, and of bringing the sands of the east to the west.

The *shabti* figure answers, 'I am here and will come wherever you bid me.'

Hymn to Ra when he rises

Another hymn of praise to the Disk of the Sun on his daily journey through the heavens,
in the Atet boat of morning and the Sektet boat of evening.

Hail, Disk, lord of rays, who rise on the horizon day by day! Shine with your beams of
light upon the face of Osiris Ani, who is victorious; for he sings hymns of praise to you
at dawn, and he makes you to set at eventide with words of adoration. May the soul
of Osiris Ani, the triumphant one, come forth with you into heaven, may he go forth
in the *Matet* boat. May he come into port in the *Sektet* boat, and may he cleave his path
among the never-resting stars in the heavens.

Osiris Ani, being in peace and in triumph, adores his lord, the lord of eternity,
saying: 'Homage to you, O Heru-khuti, who are the god Khepera, the self-created;
when you rise on the horizon and shed your beams of light upon the lands of the North
and of the South, you are beautiful, beautiful, and all the gods rejoice when they behold
you, the King of heaven. The goddess Nebt-Unnut is established upon your head; and
her uraei of the South and of the North are upon your brow; she takes up her place
before you. The god Thoth is established in the bows of your boat to destroy utterly
all your foes. Those who are in the underworld come forth to meet you, and they bow
in homage as they come towards you, to behold your beautiful Image. And I have come
before you to be with you to behold your Disk every day. May I not be shut up in the
tomb, may I not be turned back, may the limbs of my body be made new again when
I view your beauties, even as are those of all your favoured ones, because I am one of
those who worshipped you while I lived upon earth. May I come in to the land of
eternity, may I come even to the everlasting land, for behold, O my lord, this you have
ordained for me.'

And see, Osiris Ani triumphant in peace, the triumphant one, says: 'Homage to
you, O you who rise in your horizon as Ra, you repose upon law which does not

change nor can it be altered. You pass over the sky, and every face watches you and your course, for you have been hidden from their gaze. You show yourself at dawn and at eventide day by day. The *Sektet* boat, wherein is your Majesty, goes forth with might; your beams shine upon all faces; the number of your red and yellow rays cannot be known, nor can your bright beams be depicted. The lands of the gods, and the eastern lands of Punt must be seen before they can be described and before that which is hidden in you may be measured. Alone and by yourself you manifest yourself when you come into being above the sky. May Ani advance, even as you advance; may he never cease to go forward, even as your Majesty does not cease to go forward, even though it be for a moment; for with strides in one little moment you pass over the spaces which would need hundreds of thousands and millions of years for man to pass over; this you do, and then you sink to rest. You put an end to the hours of the night, and you count them, even you; you end them in your own appointed season, and the earth becomes light. You set yourself before your handiwork in the likeness of Ra; you rise in the horizon.'

Osiris Ani, triumphant, says: 'A hymn of praise to you, O you who rise like gold, and who flood the world with light on the day of your birth. Your mother gives you birth upon her hand, and you give light to the course of the Disk. O you great Light that shines in the heavens, you strengthen the generations of men with the Nile-flood, and you cause gladness in all lands, and in all cities, and in all the temples. You are glorious by reason of your splendours, and you make strong your *Ka*, with celestial foods. O you who are the mighty one of victories, you who are the power of all Powers, who strengthens your throne against evil fiends; who are glorious in majesty in the *Sektet* boat, and who are exceeding mighty in the *Atet* boat, make Osiris Ani glorious with victory in the underworld; grant that in the netherworld he may be without evil. I pray you to put away his faults behind you: grant that he may be one of

74

your venerable servants who are with the shining ones; may he be joined to the souls which are in Ta-tchesertet; and may he journey into the Sekhet-Aaru by a prosperous and happy decree, he the Osiris, the scribe, Ani, triumphant.'

Giving a Heart to Osiris

Osiris, killed and mutilated on earth, rises again to become king of the Underworld and judge of the dead. His body is reconstituted and he is given back his heart.

May my heart (*ab*) be with me in the House of Hearts! May my heart (*hat*) be with me in the House of Hearts! May my heart be with me, and may it rest there, or I shall not eat of the cakes of Osiris on the eastern side of the Lake of Flowers, neither shall I have a boat in which to go down the Nile, nor another in which to go up, nor shall I be able to sail down the Nile with you. May my mouth be given to me that I may speak with it, and my two legs to walk with, and my two hands and arms to overthrow my foe. May the doors of heaven be opened to me; may Seb, the Prince of the gods, open wide his two jaws to me; may he open my two eyes which are blindfolded; may he cause me to stretch apart my two legs which are bound together; and may Anubis make my thighs firm so that I may stand upon them. May the goddess Sekhet make me rise so that I may ascend to heaven, and so that what I command in the House of the *Ka* of Ptah may be done. I understand with my heart. I have gained the mastery over my heart, I have gained the mastery over my two hands, I have gained the mastery over my legs, I have gained the power to do whatever my *Ka* pleases. My soul shall not be fettered to my body at the gates of the underworld; but I shall enter in peace and I shall come forth in peace.

Repulsing Crocodiles

The evil Crocodile comes to carry away a magic charm, and is beaten back by Amen-hetep, son of the overseer of the house.

Get you back, return, get you back, you crocodile-fiend Sui; you shall not advance towards me, for I live by reason of the magical words which I have by me. I do not utter that name of yours to the great god who will cause you to come to the two divine envoys; the name of the one is Betti ('He of two teeth'), and the name of the other is Hra-k-en-Maat ('Your face is of right and truth'). Heaven has power over its seasons, and the magical word has power over that which is in its possession, let therefore my mouth have power over the magical word which is in it. My front teeth are like flint knives, and my back teeth are like the Nome of Tutef. Hail, you that sit with your eyeball upon these my magical words! You shall not carry them away, O you crocodile that lives by means of magical words!

Snuffing the Air

The deceased enjoys the air, growing like the Magic Egg.

Hail, you sycamore tree of the goddess Nut! Grant me a portion of the water and the air which dwell in you. I embrace the throne which is in Unnu, and I watch and guard the Egg of Nekek-ur (the Great Cackler). It grows, I grow; it lives, I live; it snuffs the air, I snuff the air, I the Osiris Ani, in triumph.

Coming Forth by Day in the Underworld

The dead come victorious into the blissful world of the Afterlife, protected by Nebseni, the lord of reverence.

I am Yesterday, Today and Tomorrow, and I have the power to be born a second time; I am the divine hidden Soul who creates the gods, and who gives celestial meals to the denizens of the underworld, Amentet, and heaven. I am the Rudder of the East, the Possessor of two Divine Faces in which his beams are seen. I am the Lord of the men who are raised up; the Lord who comes forth from out of the darkness, and whose forms of existence are of the house in which are the dead. Hail, you two Hawks who are perched upon your resting-places, who hearken to the things which are said by him, who guide the bier to the hidden place, who lead along Ra, and who follow him into the uppermost place of the shrine which is in the celestial heights! Hail, Lord of the Shrine which stands in the middle of the earth. He is I, and I am he, and Ptah has covered his sky with crystal. Hail Ra, you who are content, your heart is glad by reason of your beautiful law of the day; you enter in by Khemennu and come forth at the east, and the divine first-born beings who are in your presence cry out with gladness to you. Make your roads glad for me, and make broad for me your paths when I shall set out from earth for life in the celestial regions. Send forth your light upon me, O Soul unknown, for I am one of those who are about to enter in, and the divine speech is in my ears in the underworld, and let no defects of my mother be imputed to me; let me be delivered and let me be safe from him whose divine eyes sleep at eventide, when he gathers together and finishes the day in night.

May the Ur-urti goddesses grant such gifts to me when my tears start from me as I see myself journeying at the divine festival of Tena in Abydos, and the wooden fastenings which fasten the four doors above you are in your power within your garment. Your face is like that of a greyhound which scents with his nose the place whither I go on my feet. The god Akau transports me to the chamber, and my nurse is the divine double Lion-god himself. I am made strong and I come forth like him that forces a way through the gate, and the radiance which my heart has made is enduring; 'I know the abysses' is your name.

RUBRIC: If this chapter be known by the deceased, he shall be victorious both upon earth and in the underworld. He shall do whatever a man does who is upon the earth, and he shall perform all the deeds which those do who are alive. Now it is a great protection given by the god. This chapter was found in the city of Khemennu inscribed in letters of lapis-lazuli upon the block of iron which was under the feet of this god.

Seizing the Winds

The deceased rejoices in his righteous conduct, which endows him with power.

I have sacrificed to An-heri-ertitsa, and I am decreed to be strengthened in heart, for I have made offerings at the altars of my divine father Osiris; I rule in Tattu and I lift myself up over his land. I sniff the wind of the east by its hair; I lay hold upon the north wind by its hair; I seize and hold fast to the west wind by its body, and I go round about heaven on its four sides; I lay hold upon the south wind by its eye, and I bestow air upon the venerable beings who are in the underworld along with the eating of cakes.

RUBRIC: If this composition shall be known by the deceased upon earth he shall come forth by day, and he shall have the faculty of travelling about among the living, and his name shall never perish.

The Transformation into a Hawk of Gold

The deceased by his virtues is able to transform himself into the shape of a hawk, the divine consort of the goddess Meh-urt, and return to the world of the living.

I have risen, I have risen like the mighty hawk of gold that comes forth from his egg; I fly and I alight like the hawk which has a back four cubits wide, and the wings of which are like the mother-of-emerald of the south. I have come from the interior of the *Sektet* boat, and my heart has been brought to me from the mountain of the east. I have alighted upon the *Atet* boat, and those who were dwelling in their companies have been brought to me, and they bowed low in paying homage to me and in saluting me with cries of joy. I have risen, and I have gathered myself together like the beautiful hawk of gold, which has the head of a *Bennu* bird, and Ra enters in day by day to hearken to my words; I have taken my seat among those first-born gods of Nut. I am established, and the divine Sekhet-hetep is before me, I have eaten there, I have become a spirit there, I have an abundance there — as much as I desire — the god Nepra has given me my throat, and I have gained mastery over that which belongs to my head.

The Transformation into a Crocodile

To return to the world the transformation may take the shape of other birds and beasts, such as the dreaded Crocodile.

I am the divine crocodile which dwells in his terror, I am the divine crocodile, and I seize my prey like a ravening beast. I am the great and mighty Fish which is in the city of Qem-ur. I am the lord to whom bowing and prostrations are made in the city of Sekhem.

Knowing the Souls of the East

The deceased acknowledges the god Horus, in his personification as Heru-khuti, and the other divine Souls of the East as he describes the divine city awaiting him.

I, even I, know the eastern gate of heaven — now its southern part is at the Lake of Kharu and its northern part is at the canal of the geese — whence Ra comes with winds which make him advance. I am he who is concerned with the tackle which is in the divine bark, I am the sailor who never ceases in the boat of Ra. I, even I, know the two Sycamores of turquoise between which Ra shows himself when he strides forward over the supports of Shu towards the gate of the lord of the East through which Ra comes forth. I, even I, know the Sekhet-Aarru of Ra, the walls of which are of iron. The height of the wheat there is five cubits, of the ears two cubits, and of the stalks

three cubits. The barley is in height seven cubits, the ears are three cubits, and the stalks are four cubits. And behold, the *Khus*, each one of whom is nine cubits in height, reap it near the divine Souls of the East. I, even I, know the divine Souls of the East, that is to say, Heru-khuti, and the calf of the goddess Khera, and the Morning Star daily. A divine city has been built for me, I know it, and I know the name of it; Sekhet-Aarru is its name.

The Elysian Fields

The Fields of Peace or Fields of Reeds that await the dead are divided into many different sections, with numerous beautiful pools in which they may bathe.

Obstacles have been set before me, but I have gathered together what he has emitted. I am in my city. O Nut-urt, I have entered you, and I have counted my harvest, and I go forward to Uakh. I am the Bull enveloped in turquoise, the lord of the Field of the Bull, the lord of the divine speech of the goddess Septet at her hours. O Uakh, I have entered you, I have eaten my bread, I have gained the mastery over choice pieces of the flesh of oxen and of feathered fowl, and the birds of Shu have been given to me; I follow after the gods and I come after the divine *kas*. O Tchefet, I have entered you. I array myself in apparel, and I gird myself with the *sa* garment of Ra; now, behold, he is in heaven, and those who dwell there follow Ra, and I follow Ra in heaven. O Unen-em-hetep, lord of the two lands, I have entered you, and I have plunged into the lakes of Tchesert; behold me, for all filth has departed from me. The Great God grows there, and behold, I have found food there; I have snared feathered fowl and I feed upon the finest of them. O Qen-qentet, I have entered you, and I have seen Osiris my father, and I have gazed upon my mother, and I have made love. I have caught worms and serpents, and I am delivered. And I know the name of the god who is opposite the goddess Tchesert, and who has straight hair and is equipped with two horns; he reaps, and I both plough and reap. O Hast, I have entered you, I have driven back those who would come to the turquoise sky, and I have followed the winds of the company of the gods. The Great God has given my head to me, and he who has bound my head on me is the Mighty one who has turquoise eyes, namely, Ari-en-ab-f ('He does as he pleases'). O Usert, I have come into you at the head of the house where divine food is brought for me. O Smam, I have come into you. My heart watches, my head is equipped with the white crown, I am led into celestial regions, and I make terrestrial objects flourish, and there is joy of heart for the Bull, and for celestial beings, and for the company of the gods. I am the god who is the Bull, the lord of the gods, as he goes forth from the turquoise sky. O divine Nome of wheat and barley, I have come into you, I have come forward to you, and I have taken up that which follows me, namely, the best of the libations of the company of the gods. I have tied up my boat in the celestial lakes, I have lifted up the post at which to anchor, I have recited the prescribed words with my voice, and I have ascribed praises to the gods who dwell in Sekhet-hetep.

Address to Osiris

A prayer to be said on entering the Divine Hall of Double Maati, the Judgement Hall of Right and Wrong, to cleanse away all sin and allow the deceased to behold the faces of the gods.
Homage to you, O Great God, you lord of double Maati, I have come to you, O my Lord, and I have brought myself here that I may behold your beauties. I know you, and I know your name, and I know the names of the forty-two gods who exist with you in this Hall of double Maati, who live as warders of sinners and who feed upon their blood on the day when the lives of men are taken into account in the presence of the god Un-nefer; in truth Rekhti-merti-neb-Maati ('Twin-sisters with two eyes, ladies of double Maati') is your name. In truth I have come to you, and I have brought Maat (i.e. right and truth) to you, and I have destroyed wickedness for you. I have not done

evil to mankind. I have not oppressed the members of my family, I have not wrought evil in the place of right and truth. I have had no knowledge of worthless men. I have not wrought evil. I have not made the first consideration of each day that excessive labour should be performed for me. I have not brought forward my name for exaltation to honours. I have not ill-treated servants. I have not thought scorn of God. I have not defrauded the oppressed one of his property. I have not done that which is an abomination to the gods. I have not caused harm to be done to the servant by his chief. I have not caused pain. I have made no man suffer hunger. I have made no one weep. I have done no murder. I have not given the order for murder to be done for me. I have not inflicted pain upon mankind. I have not defrauded the temples of their oblations. I have not purloined the cakes of the gods. I have not carried off the cakes offered to the *khus*. I have not committed fornication. I have not polluted myself in the holy places of the god of my city, nor diminished from the bushel. I have neither added to nor filched away land. I have not encroached upon the fields of others. I have not added to the weights of the scales to cheat the seller. I have not mis-read the pointer of the scales to cheat the buyer. I have not carried away the milk from the mouths of children. I have not driven away the cattle which were upon their pastures. I have not snared the feathered fowl of the preserves of the gods. I have not caught fish with bait made of fish of their kind. I have not turned back the water at the time when it should flow. I have not cut a cutting in a canal of running water. I have not extinguished a fire when it should burn. I have not violated the times of offering the chosen meat-offerings. I have not driven off the cattle from the property of the gods. I have not repulsed God in his manifestations. I am pure. My purity is the purity of that great *Bennu* which is in the city of Suten-henen, for behold, I am the nose of the God of the winds, who makes all mankind to live on the day when the Eye of Ra is full in Annu at the end of the second month of the season *Pert* (the season of growing) in the presence of the divine lord of this earth. I have seen the Eye of Ra when it was full in Annu, therefore let not evil befall me in this land and in this Hall of double Maati, because I, even I, know the names of these gods who are here and who are the followers of the great god.

The Circle of Bright Flame

Osiris declares his virtues and the accomplishment of his great deeds.

Hail, bright and shining flames which keep your place behind Ra, and which slay behind him, the boat of Ra is in fear of the whirlwind and the storm; shine forth, then, and make yourselves visible. I have come daily along with the god Sek-hra from the bight of his holy lake, and I have seen the Maat goddesses pass along, and the Lion-gods who belong to them. Hail, you that dwell in the coffer, who have multitudes of plants, I have seen what is there. We rejoice, and their princes rejoice greatly, and their lesser gods are glad. I have made a way in front of the boat of Ra, I have lifted myself up into his divine Disk, I shine brightly through his splendours; he has furnished himself with the things which are his, taking possession of them as the lord of right and truth. Behold, come, come, and declare before him the testimony of right and truth of the lord Tem. I cry out at eventide and at his hour, saying: Grant me that I may come. I have brought to him the jaws of the passages of the tomb; I have brought to him the bones which are in Annu; I have gathered together for him his manifold parts; I have driven back for him the serpent fiend Apep; I have spat upon his gashes for him; I have made my road and I have passed in among you. I am he who dwells among the gods, come, let me pass onwards in the boat, the boat of the lord Sa. Behold, O Heru-ur, there is a flame, but the fire has been extinguished. I have made my road, O you divine fathers and your divine apes! I have entered upon the horizon, and I have passed on to the side of the divine princes, and I have borne testimony to him that dwells in his divine boat. I have gone forward over the circle of bright flame which is behind the lord of the lock of hair which moves round about. Behold, you who cry out over yourselves, you worms in your hidden places, grant that I may pass onwards, for I am the mighty one, the lord of divine strength, and I am the spiritual body of the lord of divine right and truth made by the goddess Uatchit. His strength which protects is my strength which protects, which is the strength which protects Ra. Grant that I may be in the following of Ra, and grant that I may go round about with him in Sekhet-hetep and in the two lands. I am a great god, and I have been judged by the company of his gods; grant that divine, sepulchral meals may be given to me.

The Book of the Full Utchat

The Utchat or eye of the Full Moon, Horus's eye, restored after his fight with the evil Set, is a symbol of great power.

The divine Power has risen that shines in the horizon, and the god Tem has risen out of the odour of that which flows from him. The *Khus* shine in heaven and Het-benbenet rejoices, for there is among them a form which is like themselves; and there are shouts and cries of gladness within the shrine, and the sounds of those who rejoice go round about through the underworld, and homage is paid to him at the decree of Tem and Heru-khuti. His Majesty orders the company of the gods to follow in the train of his Majesty; his Majesty orders the calling of the *Utchat* with you to my members. He has given strength to all my limbs, and has made them vigorous with that which comes forth from the mouth of His Majesty. His divine Eye rests upon its seat with His Majesty at that hour of the night on the day of the fulfilment of the fourth hour of the beautiful land, on the last day of the second month of the season *pert*. The Majesty of the *Utchat* is in the presence of the company of the gods, and His Majesty shines as he shone in the primeval time, when the *Utchat* was first upon his head. The computation of the *Utchat* has been made in the presence of the divine lord of this earth; it is full to the uttermost, and it rests. And these gods are rejoicing on this day, and they have their hands beneath them, and the festival of every god having been celebrated, they say: 'Hail, praise be to you, O you who are as Ra, rejoice in him, for the mariners of his boat sail round about, and he has overthrown the fiend Apep. Hail, praise be to you, O you who are as Ra who makes himself come into being in the form of the god Khepera. Hail, praise be to you, O you who are as Ra, for he has destroyed his enemies. Hail, praise be to Ra, for he has crushed the heads of the children of impotent rebellion. And praise and rejoicing be to the Osiris Auf-ankh, triumphant.'

RUBRIC: This chapter shall be recited over an *Utchat* of real lapis-lazuli or of *mak* stone plated with gold, before which shall be offered every kind of fair and pure oblation when Ra shows himself on the last day of the second month of the season *pert*. And you shall make another *Utchat* of jasper and place it upon such part of the dead man's body as you please, and when this chapter has been recited before the boat of Ra, the deceased shall be borne along with these gods, and he shall become one of them, and he shall be made to rise up in the underworld. And while this chapter is being recited, and likewise while the offerings are being made at the time when the *Utchat* is full, four altars shall be lighted for Ra-Tem, and four for the *Utchat*, and four for the gods who have been mentioned. And upon each one of them there shall be bread-cakes made of fine flour, and five white cakes, and plants, and *shai*, and five *baaq*, and of incense one measure, and of *teq* incense one measure, and one roasted joint of meat.

Entering the Mansions

Osiris in one of his personifications shows his might. The rubric lists the benefits the deceased will accrue from reciting these words.

The Osiris Nu makes a way through the firmament, he drives away the whirlwind and the storm, he makes the mariners of Ra live, and he makes offerings come to the place where he is. The Osiris Nu causes a boat to be made, he travels happily in it; the Osiris Nu makes a way and he advances on it. The face of the Osiris Nu is like that of the god Ur-pehi-f by reason of its might, and the Osiris Nu is the lord of might. The Osiris Nu is at rest in the horizon, and he is valiant to overthrow you, O ye *Nehesu* gods; make a path, then, for your lord Osiris.

RUBRIC: This chapter shall be said over a drawing of the divine sovereign chiefs, which has been done in yellow ink, on the boat of Ra; and offerings and oblations shall be made to them, and sacrifices of feathered fowl, and incense shall be burnt before them. These acts will make the deceased live, and they will give him strength among these gods, and he shall neither be repulsed nor turned back at the pylons of the underworld. And, moreover, you shall make a figure of the deceased in their presence, and you shall make it come forth towards every one of these gates which are painted above. And you shall recite this chapter at the door of each of the Arits which are painted above, and at each one of them you shall make offerings, the thigh, the head, the heart, and the hoof of a red bull; and four vessels of blood which has not come from the breast; and amulets; and sixteen loaves of white bread, and eight *pasen* loaves, and eight *shenen* loaves, and eight *khenfu* loaves, and eight *hebennu* loaves, and eight large vessels of beer, and eight large vessels of grain; and four earthenware vessels filled with the milk of a white cow, and fresh herbs, and fresh olives, and unguent, and eye-paint, and *hatet* unguent, and incense to be burnt on the fire, and this chapter shall be recited twice over each earthenware vessel, after the image has been made, at the fourth hour, going round about by day; and take good heed to the time in the heavens. Now when you do what is written in this book do not allow any person whatever to see you. And this ceremony shall make long the strides of the deceased in heaven, and on earth, and in the underworld, and it shall benefit him in everything he does, and he shall possess the things of the day regularly and continually.

A Buckle of Carnelian

A prayer that invests with protective powers the jewel placed on the body of the deceased at his funeral.

May the blood of Isis, and the powers of Isis, and the enchantments of Isis be powers to protect this mighty one and to guard him from him that would do him anything which he abominates.

RUBRIC: This chapter shall be said over a buckle of carnelian, which has been steeped in water of *ankhami* flowers, and set in a plinth of sycamore wood, and it shall be placed at the neck of the deceased on the day of the funeral. If these things be done for him the powers of Isis shall protect his limbs, and Horus the son of Isis shall rejoice in him, when he sees him; and there shall be no hidden places on his path, and one hand shall be towards heaven, and one hand shall be towards earth, regularly and continually. You shall not let any person who is with you see it.

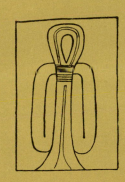

Entrance into Heaven

The god Thoth eases the path for the deceased by addressing the Doors into Heaven.

I   To the Door of the west wind. 'Ra lives, the Tortoise dies. Pure is the body in the earth, and pure are the bones of Osiris the *am-khent*, Nefer-uben-f, triumphant.'

II To the Door of the east wind. 'Ra lives, the Tortoise dies. Sound is he who is in the chest, who is in the chest, Osiris Nefer-uben-f, triumphant.'

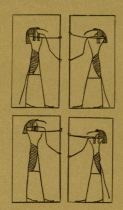

III To the Door of the north wind. 'Ra lives, the Tortoise dies. The Osiris Nefer-
uben-f, triumphant, is strong in his members, Qebh-sennuf guards them.'
IV To the Door of the south wind. 'Ra lives, the Tortoise dies. The bolts are drawn
and they pass through his foundation.'

RUBRIC: Every *sahu* for whom these divine figures have been painted upon his coffin
shall make his way through these four entrances into heaven. That of the north wind
belongs to Osiris; that of the south wind to Ra; that of the west wind to Isis; and that
of the east wind to Nephthys. Each one of these winds shall breathe into his nostrils
as he enters in his daily course. Let none who is outside know this chapter; it is a great
mystery, and those who dwell in the swamps (i.e. the ignorant) do not know it. You
shall not do this in the presence of any person except your father or your son, or
yourself alone; for it is, indeed, an exceedingly great mystery which no man
whatsoever knows.

Making Heat to be under the Head of the Deceased

The Cow, mother of Ra, asks for the head of the deceased to be warmed as it was in life.
Homage to you, O you god Par, you mighty one, whose plumes are lofty, you lord
of the *Ureret* crown, who rule with the whip; you are the lord of the phallus, you
grow as you shine with rays of light, and your shining is to the uttermost parts of
earth and sky. You are the lord of transformations, and have manifold skins, which
you hide in the *Utchat* at its birth. You are the mighty one of names among the gods,
the mighty runner whose strides are mighty; you are the god, the mighty one who
comes and rescues the needy one and the afflicted from him that oppresses him;
give heed to my cry. I am the Cow, and your divine name is in my mouth, and I will

88

utter it. I praise your name. I am the Cow that hearkens to the petition on the day when you place heat under the head of Ra. O place it for him in the divine gate in Annu, and you shall make him become even like him that is upon the earth; he is your soul… O be gracious to Osiris Auf-ankh, triumphant, and cause your heat to exist under his head, for, indeed, he is the soul of the great divine Body which rests in Annu. Be gracious, then, and grant that he may become like one of those who are in your following, for he is even as are you.

RUBRIC: This chapter shall be recited over the image of a cow which has been made in fine gold and placed at the neck of the deceased, and it shall be written upon new papyrus and placed under his head, then abundant warmth shall be in him throughout, even like that in him when he was upon earth. This has exceedingly great protective power, for it was made by the cow for her son Ra when he was setting and when his habitation was surrounded by a company of beings of fire. And the deceased shall become divine in the underworld, and he shall never be turned back at any of its gates.

And you shall say when you place the image of this goddess at the neck of the deceased: 'O Amen, O Amen, who are in heaven, turn your face upon the dead body of your son and make him sound and strong in the underworld.' This is a composition of exceedingly great mystery. Let not the eye of any man whatsoever see it, for it is an abominable thing for every man to know it; therefore hide it. "Book of the mistress of the hidden temple" is its name.'

Thoth Repulses the Foes of Osiris

Osiris is protected, strengthened and guarded in the Underworld by the operation of the will of Thoth, divine originator of the world.

I am Thoth, the perfect scribe, whose hands are pure, the lord of the two horns, who destroys iniquity, the scribe of right and truth, who abominates sin. Behold, he is the writing-reed of the god Neb-er-tcher, the lord of laws, who gives forth the speech of wisdom and understanding, whose words have dominion over the two lands. I am Thoth, the lord of right and truth, who tries the right and the truth for the gods, the judge of words in their essence, whose words triumph over violence. I have scattered the darkness, I have driven away the whirlwind and the storm, and I have given the pleasant breeze of the north wind to Osiris Un-nefer as he came forth from the womb of her who gave him birth. I have made Ra to set as Osiris, and Osiris sets as Ra sets. I have made him enter the hidden habitation to vivify the heart of the Still-Heart, the holy Soul, who dwells in Amentet, and to shout cries of joy to the Still-Heart, Un-nefer, the son of Nut.

I am Thoth, the favoured one of Ra, the lord of might, who brings to a prosperous end that which he does, the mighty one of enchantments who is in the boat of millions of years, the lord of laws, the subduer of the two lands, whose words of might gave strength to her that gave him birth, whose word does away with opposition and fighting, and who performs the will of Ra in his shrine.

I am Thoth, who caused Osiris to triumph over his enemies.

I am Thoth, who issues the decree at dawn, whose sight follows on again after his overthrow at his season, the guide of heaven, and earth, and the underworld, and the creator of the life of all nations and peoples. I gave air to him that was in the hidden place by means of the might of the magical words of my utterance, and Osiris triumphed over his enemies. I came to you, O lord of Ta-tcheser, Osiris, Bull of Ament, and you were strengthened for ever. I set everlastingness as a protection for your members, and I came to you having protection in my hand, and I guarded you with strength during the course of each and every day; protection and life were behind this god, and his *Ka* was glorified with power.

The king of the Underworld, the prince of Amentat, the victorious conqueror of heaven, has the *Atef* crown firmly established upon him, he is diademed with the white crown, and he grasps the crook and the whip; to him, the great one of souls, the mighty one of the *Ureret* crown, every god is gathered together, and love for him who is Un-nefer, and whose existence is for everlasting and all eternity, goes through their bodies.

I am Thoth, and I have pacified Horus, and I have quieted the two divine Combatants in their season of storm. I have come and I have washed the Ruddy one, I have quieted the Stormy one, and I have filled him with all manner of evil things.

I am Thoth, and I have made the 'things of the night' in Sekhem.

I am Thoth, and I have come daily into the cities of Pe and Tepu. I have led along the offerings and oblations, I have given cakes with lavish hand to the *Khus*, I have protected the shoulder of Osiris, I have embalmed him, I have made sweet his odour, even as is that of the beautiful god.

I am Thoth, and I have come each day into the city of Kher-aha. I have tied the cordage and I have set in good order the Makhent boat, and I have brought it from the East to the West. I am more exalted upon my standard than any god in my name of 'He whose face is exalted'. I have opened fair things in my name of Ap-uat (Opener of the road), and I have ascribed praise and done homage to Osiris Un-nefer, whose existence is for ever and for ever.

Glossary

ab: the heart, the preservation of which was of the greatest importance.

Abtu, **Ant**: the fish that swim at the bows of the sun-god's boat.

Abtu: the city of Abydos.

Akau: another name for Anubis.

Akert: one of the names of the underworld.

Ament: the abode of the dead, on the west bank of the Nile.

am-khent: a priestly title of Osiris.

An: one of the names of the sun-god.

Annu: the city of Helio-polis, dedicated to Ra.

Anubis: the jackal-headed god of the dead who supervised the weighing of souls and the embalming of the body.

Apep: enemy of Horus and Ra.

Atet boat: the boat of the morning sun.

ba: the soul, dwelling with the **ka** in the tomb; sometimes depicted as a human-headed hawk.

Bennu: phoenix.

Geb: one of the nine chief gods.

hat: the chest or breast area of the body.

Heru-khuti: Horus of the two horizons, Manu and Bakhatet.

Horus: god of the sun and of kingship, personified as a falcon. His eyes were the sun and moon, and the moon eye was damaged in a fight with Set (the explanation for the moon's phases) and healed by Thoth. The emblem of the restored **utchat** eye became a powerful amulet.

Isis: goddess of healing and protection, personifying motherhood.

Ka: the double of the deceased, which could wander at will from the tomb.

khaibit: the shadow, closely associated with the soul.

khat: the physical body, which could be preserved only by mummification.

Khemennu: the city of Hermopolis.

Khepera: god of the rising sun, seated in the **Atet** boat; the god of dead matter about to burst into life.

khu: the spirit, dwelling in the spiritual body or **sahu**.

Maat: goddess of order and truth; wife of Thoth, daughter of Ra. Her emblem is the feather.

Manu: the mountain where the sun sets in the west. The eastern mountain where he rises is Bakhatet.

Neb-er-tcher: 'Lord of All', a name for Osiris after his magical reconstruction.

Nebt-Unnut: 'the lady of the hour'.

Nephthys: the wife of Set; one of the nine chief gods and goddesses.

Nome: a district, province or metropolitan area with a local governor.

Nut: goddess of the sky, arched over the earth.

Nut-urt: one of the pools in the 'Elysian Fields' or Fields of Reeds.

Osiris: god of the dead, brother and husband of Isis; father of Horus. Killed by his brother Set, his body was miraculously reconstructed by his wife and he became ruler and judge of the underworld. He symbolises immortality; the deceased identifies himself with Osiris in hope of resurrection.

Pert: the sixth month of the Egyptian year.

Ptah: creator god, patron of craftsmen. His city was Memphis.

Punt: the land in the Horn of Africa.

pylon: monumental gateway.

Qenqentet: one of the pools in the 'Elysian Fields' or Fields of Reeds.

Ra or **Re**: god of the sun, who sails across the earth by day and through the underworld by night.

ren: the name of the deceased, the preservation of which was essential.

sahu: the spiritual body, the habitation of the soul.

Seb the Erpat: husband of Nut, father of Osiris, Isis, Set, Nephthys and Horus; ancestor of the gods (same as **Geb**).

Seker: 'He who is in his coffin'.

sehkem: the power or vital force of the deceased.

Sekhet-Hetepu, Aru: the 'Elysian Fields' or Fields of Reeds; a region of these.

Sektet boat: the boat of the setting sun.

Set or **Setekh**: god who murdered his brother Osiris and was killed by Osiris' son Horus; the embodiment of evil.

shabti: little figures in a tomb, 'slaves' intended to work for the deceased in the afterlife.

Shenit: divine officials.

Shu: one of the nine chief gods; supports of Shu: the four pillars at the North, South, East and West corners of heaven.

Smam: one of the pools in the 'Elysian Fields' or Fields of Reeds.

Ta-her-sta-nef: 'He leads the earth'.

Ta-tchesert: one of the names of the underworld.

Tatunen: god of the earth.

Tchatcha: heads or chiefs.

Tchefet: a district in the 'Elysian Fields' or Fields of Reeds.

Tefnut: one of the nine chief gods.

Tem: another name for the sun-god.

Thoth: divine originator of the world; scribe of the gods and inventor of arts and sciences.

Tuat: the underworld.

Uakh: one of the pools in the 'Elysian Fields' or Fields of Reeds.

Uraeus: the sacred serpent emblem found on the headdresses of kings and gods. There were two, one for the North and one for the South kingdom.

Ur-urti: the goddesses Isis and Nephthys.

Usert: one of the pools in the 'Elysian Fields' or Fields of Reeds.

Utchat: the eye of the full moon; *see* **Horus**.

The Pictures

95

Sir Ernest Wallis Budge (1857–1934) was an Assyriologist and Egyptologist who studied at Christ's College, Cambridge, and became Keeper of the Department of Egyptian and Syrian Antiquities at the British Museum from 1894 to 1924. He edited the standard text of the *Book of the Dead*, from which these excerpts are taken. He was knighted in 1920.

96

First published in the United Kingdom in 2001 by Cassell & Co
Introduction and text copyright © Estate of E.A. Wallis Budge Permission to reproduce copyright material has been granted by the Master and Fellows of Christ's College, Cambridge, and University College, Oxford.
Design and layout copyright © Cassell & Co, 2001

The picture acknowledgements on pages 94/95 constitute an extension of this copyright page. Distributed in the United States of America by Sterling Publishing Co. Inc.

A CIP catalogue record for this book is available from the British Library.

ISBN 0 304 356190

Design Director David Rowley
Case designed by Senate
Designed by Nigel Soper
Project manager Elisabeth Ingles
Printed and bound in Trento, Italy

Cassell & Co
Wellington House
125 Strand
London
WC2R 0BB